DATE DUE

SE 23 '85			
4			
SEP 2 7 1988			
Smith			

DEMCO 38-297

The New
Enchantment of America
ILLINOIS

By Allan Carpenter

 CHILDRENS PRESS, CHICAGO

ACKNOWLEDGMENTS

For assistance in the preparation of the revised edition, the author thanks:
GOJAN NIKOLICH, Office of Tourists, Illinois Department of Business and Economic Development; ALLEN D. GOLDHAMER, Director of Public Relations, Chicago Convention and Tourism Bureau; and GLENN W. HARPER, Supervisor, Illinois Department of Conservation.

American Airlines—Anne Vitaliano, Director of Public Relations; *Capitol Historical Society,* Washington, D.C.; *Newberry Library,* Chicago, Dr. Lawrence Towner, Director; *Northwestern University Library,* Evanston, Illinois; *United Airlines*—John P. Grember, Manager of Special Promotions; Joseph P. Hopkins, Manager, News Bureau; Carl Provorse, *Carpenter Publishing House.*

UNITED STATES GOVERNMENT AGENCIES: *Department of Agriculture*—Robert Hailstock, Jr., Photography Division, Office of Communication; Donald C. Schuhart, Information Division, Soil Conservation Service. *Army*—Doran Topolosky, Public Affairs Office, Chief of Engineers, Corps of Engineers. *Department of Interior*—Louis Churchville, Director of Communications; EROS Space Program—Phillis Wiepking, Community Affairs; Charles Withington, Geologist; Mrs. Ruth Herbert, Information Specialist; Bureau of Reclamation; National Park Service—Fred Bell and the individual sites; Fish and Wildlife Service—Bob Hines, Public Affairs Office. *Library of Congress*—Dr. Alan Fern, Director of the Department of Research; Sara Wallace, Director of Publications; Dr. Walter W. Ristow, Chief, Geography and Map Division; Herbert Sandborn, Exhibits Officer. *National Archives*—Dr. James B. Rhoads, Archivist of the United States; Albert Meisel, Assistant Archivist for Educational Programs; David Eggenberger, Publications Director; Bill Leary, Still Picture Reference; James Moore, Audio-Visual Archives. *United States Postal Service*—Herb Harris, Stamps Division.

For assistance in the preparation of the first edition, the author thanks:
Consultant Sarajane Wells, Education Director, Chicago Historical Society; S.A. Wetherbee, Illinois State Historical Society; I.A. Palmer, Division of Legal Services, Illinois Department of Public Instruction; Dr. Woodson Fishback, Coordinator, Illinois Curriculum Program; Dr. Dale McDowell, Illinois Curriculum Program; Mrs. Olive S. Foster, Editor, *Illinois History;* and Mrs. Paul Rhymer, Curator of Prints, Chicago Historical Society.

Illustrations on the preceding pages:
Cover: Chicago skyline, Jim Rowan
Page 1: Commemorative stamps of historic interest
Pages 2-3: Chicago skyline at night, Chicago Convention and Tourism Bureau
Page 3: (Map) USDI Geological Survey
Pages 4-5: Chicago area and Lake Michigan, EROS Space Photo, USDI Geological Survey, EROS Data Center

Project Editor, Revised Edition:
Joan Downing
Assistant Editor, Revised Edition:
Mary Reidy

Revised Edition Copyright © 1979 by Regensteiner Publishing Enterprises, Inc. Copyright © 1963, Childrens Press, Inc. All rights reserved. Printed in the U.S.A. Published simultaneously in Canada

6 7 8 9 10 11 12 R 85 84

Library of Congress Cataloging in Publication Data

Carpenter, John Allan, 1917-
    Illinois.

    (His The new enchantment of America)
    SUMMARY: A history of the state with a view of its industries today and a profile of some famous Illinoisans.
    1. Illinois—Juvenile literature.
[1. Illinois] I. Title. II. Series.
F541.3.C29   977.3   78-32064
ISBN 0-516-04113-4

977.3
C

Contents

127531

The original Piasa Bird was ruined when the cliff it was carved
on was blasted and the rocks used to make ballast for a railroad.
A German publisher had sent Henry Lewis to Illinois in 1839 and his
sketch of the Piasa Bird (above) remains.

8

A True Story to Set the Scene

A BLUFF MONSTER

"There are great monsters in the land of the Illini; beware or they will devour you," the Indians warned Father Marquette and Louis Jolliet as they set out on the journey to discover the northern Mississippi River and the land of Illinois along its banks.

Many weeks passed, and the travelers saw no monsters and had no narrow escapes. Then, suddenly, one day they came face to face with not one monster but two.

Fortunately for the little party of travelers, the monsters turned out to be figures painted high on the bluffs overlooking the Mississippi. This is the way Marquette described it in his wonderful diary: "Passing the mouth of the Illinois River we soon fell into the shadow of a tall promontory and with great astonishment beheld representations of two monsters painted on the lofty limestone front. . . . They are painted red, green, and black and are an object of Indian Worship."

Ever since those first discoverers found them, the painted figures on the cliff have proved to be one of Illinois' great mysteries.

They appeared to be fierce animals with the wings of a bird and the claws of a lizard. No one knows what Indian group or prehistoric man may have painted them. They seemed to be the work of clever artists.

Later travelers rediscovered them and disagreed on just what they saw. Twenty-three years after Marquette, in 1699, Father de Cosme viewed the rock and found the figures much worn away. He said they seemed to be about 30 feet (9.1 meters) long and 12 feet (3.6 meters) high, with the wings of a bat.

In the early 1800s a writer said he counted 10,000 bullet holes on or near the paintings, and one of the monsters had disappeared. Apparently the superstitious Indians shot at the paintings every time they passed by. The bullets were rapidly wearing the remaining figure away.

However, in 1846 or 1847, workmen blasted the whole cliff apart

The modern version of the Piasa Bird as recreated by the people of Alton. It can be seen along the river highway near Alton.

and carted the rocks away to make ballast for a railroad. And with their ballast they carried off a relic that had made Illinois famous even at that early date.

Fortunately, a German publisher had sent the now-famous artist Henry Lewis to Illinois in 1839 and published a sketch of the remaining figure in a book called *The Valley of the Mississippi, Illustrated.* They called the figure *Piasa Bird* or *Thunderbird,* because that was the name given to similar figures in Europe.

Today if you travel along the river highway near Alton you may turn a corner and be as surprised as Marquette and Jolliet, for there is a great Piasa bird glowering down from the cliff just as it did many years ago.

The people of Alton have had a 30-foot (9.1-meter) Piasa bird reproduced as nearly as possible like the original as a reminder of one of the most interesting stories in Illinois history.

There are many such interesting stories in the history of Illinois, and many more of them are told in this book because they help explain the enchantment of Illinois.

10

Lay of the Land

What would an astronaut see, zooming across Illinois, if he had time to look out?

He would be able to see entirely across the state from Lake Michigan and the Wabash River on the east to the Mississippi River on the west. There would be a fine view from the rocky, hilly area on the northwest corner of Illinois to the hills in the southern part of the state and the very southern tip of the state—the part early settlers called *Little Egypt* because they thought it looked like the delta of the Nile in Egypt.

From so high in the air it would be simple to understand why the Chain of Lakes region on the northern border got its name. It lies like a necklace or chain of azure stones, the lakes strung on a blue string, the Fox River.

About five hundred rivers and streams would spread out in all directions below an astronaut like sparkling threads. He might even be able to identify the major rivers: the Illinois, Kaskaskia, Sangamon, Spoon, Rock, Embarrass, Kankakee, and Des Plaines.

From an astronaut's height, Illinois would appear mostly as flat as a map on a sheet of paper—so peaceful it would be hard to imagine that anything violent had ever happened there.

But it is true Nature has done a great many things to disturb the land of Illinois.

Much of the story of Nature's land building can be "read" in "books" of limestone. Shells and the hardened bodies of other animals from the sea can be seen clearly in some cut pieces of limestone or sandstone. How could creatures from the sea get into the rocks of Illinois, so far away from any ocean?

The answer is that Illinois lay at the bottom of a shallow inland ocean, not once but many times. Each time the land would rise again, little by little, until it was again above the surface of the water, bringing with it plants and animals from the sea.

Land plants and animals would begin to grow once more; then the surface would begin to sink, and Illinois, with everything on it, would end up at the bottom of the sea again.

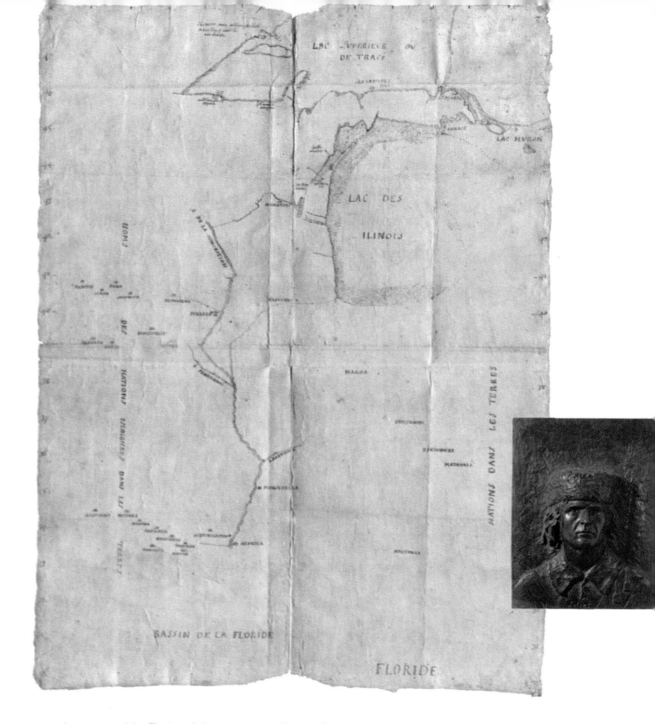

A map used by Father Marquette and Louis Jolliet, reproduced from the original in the archives of the College of Sainte-Marie in Montreal. The bust of Jolliet (inset) is a half-relief bronze plaque.

12

Garden of the Gods in Shawnee National Forest.

Each time this happened, the layers of plants and animals were buried deeper and deeper under new layers of sand and gravel, until the weight pressed the plants and animals into coal or petroleum, and the layers of sand and gravel hardened until they became sandstone or limestone.

All of this happened unimaginable millions of years in the past. Finally, about sixty million years ago, the ocean waters receded for the last time.

But Nature was not through with Illinois. No one knows why the weather became colder, but it did. Far to the north more and more snow fell. Since the snow could not melt, it grew into huge packs of ice, or glaciers.

These glaciers began to slide south, slowly crunching and grinding over almost all of Illinois. The glaciers were so heavy and powerful they leveled off the tops of hills and filled in the valleys, carrying everything in their path, including great rocks and trees. All of the material picked up by the glaciers usually was dumped miles from where it had been originally. They deposited a layer of fine soil, some of it 100 feet (30.5 meters) thick, over a large part of the state.

Then the climate turned warmer and the glaciers slowly melted. This happened four times in a row.

Only two small parts of Illinois were left untouched by the icy fingers of the glaciers—the rocky, hilly area spotted by the astronaut in the northwest corner, and Little Egypt at the very tip.

Today the land of Illinois is much as the last glacier left it.

Chicago as it appeared 300 million years ago; from a diorama at the Chicago Academy of Science. The ancestor of the dragonfly in the foreground measured 23 inches (58 centimeters) across.

Footsteps on the Land

BUILDERS OF MOUNDS

When Europeans began to come into the Illinois country, they found great mounds of dirt, many of them very long. They might have been small hills except for their shapes. Some of them were in the form of twisting serpents; others could be recognized as turtles, or birds. A few looked like the bases of pyramids. Clearly these had been made by human hands.

Curious Europeans asked the Indians, but they knew nothing about the mounds or the people who made them. Not until scholars began to excavate these mounds did anything become known about them.

Some of the mounds were burial places. Hundreds of skeletons were found in them. With the skeletons were buried tools, implements, and other things their owners might need after death. Strange things from faraway places were found to show that these people had contact with distant regions.

The pyramid-shaped mounds had been raised to support temples or other religious buildings. Still other kinds of mounds served as forts. Because of their great size, it is hard to believe that these mounds could have been formed by workers building them up with dirt carried long distances in baskets. Yet this is considered to be the only way the work could have been accomplished. Such work must have required thousands of workers, sometimes for many·years.

Of course, these early people have come to be called the *Mound Builders*. But who they were and what happened to them is still as much of a mystery as ever. Some of the later mounds seem to show that the Mound Builders were beginning to lose their skill; we have no way of knowing why. The Indians who met the first explorers and settlers were of different races than the Mound Builders. They were much more primitive in their civilization than the Mound Builders had been.

Today, more than ten thousand mounds, scattered throughout the state, still cast their spell of mystery. Monks Mound near Cahokia,

Charles S. Winslow's painting shows Father Marquette's crude winter quarters on the banks of the Chicago River in 1675.

Illinois, is believed to be the largest primitive earthwork in the world.

THE EXPLORER AND THE PRIEST

The voyage of exploration that led to the discovery of Illinois is generally thought to be one of the world's great adventure stories.

A French priest, Father Jacques Marquette, and a young French explorer, Louis Jolliet, were sent by the French governor of Canada to explore the Mississippi and, if possible, to find out where it led.

They became, as far as is known, the first Europeans to set foot in Illinois. They were the first Europeans to have contact with the Indians of Illinois. On their first meeting with the Indians, after a friendly council, the Indians treated their new friends to a feast of Indian corn, fish, and "wild ox." They could not bring themselves to eat the dishes of fried dog on the menu and found it difficult to let the Indians feed them as if they were babies.

Before he left, Marquette promised to return and teach the Indian people about Christianity, as he had so long dreamed of doing.

16

Possibly the single most important contribution made by Marquette and Jolliet to Illinois history is found in their return voyage. They decided to go back by way of the Illinois River, and so they cut through the heart of the state.

The richness of the soil and the lack of trees especially impressed them. Later Jolliet told friends in Canada that the Illinois River valley was "Most beautiful and suitable for settlement ... a settler would not there spend ten years in cutting down and burning trees; on the very day of his arrival, he could put his plow into the ground. Thus he would easily find in the country his food and clothing."

From the Illinois River, they swung their canoes into the Des Plaines River. When Marquette and Jolliet carried their canoes across the portage from the Des Plaines to the Chicago River, they were the first Europeans to follow that route, over which so many thousands were to follow. Jolliet was wise enough to foresee that the route he and Marquette had taken would some day be one of the great trade routes of the world.

Jolliet was the first to suggest cutting a canal between the Chicago and Des Plaines rivers, and this was done more than 175 years later. He must also have the credit for first seeing the rich future ahead for the country he and his friend had explored for the first time.

LAND OF "THE MEN"

Long before Jolliet saw the richness of Illinois, the Indians had known it was a good hunting ground. The Illini, found by Marquette and Jolliet, were a group of six related groups of Indians: Michigamea, Moingwena, Peoria, Tamaroa, Cahokia, and Kaskaskia. They called themselves *Illini,* which means *the men,* because they thought they were superior to other Indians. Later, the French changed this name to Illinois.

Over the years most of the Illini were killed by the fierce Iroquois Indians from the East. Other Indians came and went. The Miami lived for a while near Chicago. From time to time the Shawnee Indians appeared in southern Illinois. Early in the eighteenth century the confederated clan of the Sauk and Fox left Wisconsin to settle in Illinois. Other Indians included the Chippewa, Ottawa, Mascouten, and Piankeshaw.

The Potawatomi, who lived in northeastern Illinois, were the last Indians to leave the state.

UNDER THREE FLAGS

The French king and his governors in Canada moved ahead quickly to claim the lands found by Marquette and Jolliet.

The famous French explorer La Salle and his Italian helper, Henri de Tonti, set up forts and established a fur trade. French priests founded the town of Cahokia in 1699, and it was the first permanent European settlement in the Mississippi Valley. Kaskaskia, established in 1703, became the largest and most important of the French villages in the Illinois country. The French built many forts, including Fort de Chartres. At one time this was the strongest fort on the North American continent. Towns usually grew up around the forts.

But French settlements in Illinois grew slowly. Probably there never were more than two thousand French settlers in the whole state. Yet this small group managed to grow crops of grain that helped to feed the whole Mississippi Valley as far south as New Orleans.

Almost everywhere the French went the British went also. Wherever they met, they clashed. This competition went on all around the world. In America the conflict between British and French became what we call the French and Indian War. The Indians helped both sides. The Algonquins sided with the French; the feared Iroquois with the British.

When Britain won the French and Indian War, the last French flag to fly on the North American continent was the one at Fort de Chartres, Illinois, and it was lowered in 1765.

About the only reminder of the French in Illinois today is furnished by the names of a few towns such as La Salle, Creve Coeur, Des Plaines, Du Quoin, Marseilles, and Paris.

18

A room in one of the better French houses in Illinois as recreated by the Chicago Historical Society. The fireplace was used for cooking as well as for heating the home. Most of the furniture was handmade.

George Rogers Clark, American Revolutionary general and conqueror of the Northwest Territory.

British control of the Illinois country from 1765 to 1778 was neither very wise nor very strong. The area became almost as lawless as the "wild west" of a hundred years later.

Into this tough situation had come one of the great frontiersman of all time. Young George Rogers Clark had brought his skill with a rifle and his ability as a leader to Illinois to help protect the settlers against the Indians and the bandit groups.

Then came word in 1776 that the American colonies on the East Coast had signed a Declaration of Independence against the British.

Clark felt that he might be able to take the whole Illinois country away from England. He went to Virginia in 1777 and asked the famous governor of that state, Patrick Henry, for help with his plan. The governor gave him all the help he could, in the name of the state of Virginia.

A tiny army of only 175 men was all Clark could gather in Kentucky and Ohio, but with this small group he set out to conquer Illinois.

He reached Kaskaskia on Independence Day, 1778, just two years after the first Independence Day. He surprised the British commander, and Clark took control of the fort at Kaskaskia.

When Governor Henry heard the news, he quickly claimed the Illinois country in the name of Virginia. Illinois, strange as it seems, became a county of faraway Virginia.

But Clark knew that the British commander at Vincennes was planning to recapture Kaskaskia and bring all of the Illinois country back under British control. He was expected to move as soon as warm weather came.

Knowing that if he waited for the British attack, his small force could never hold out, Clark decided on a plan that resulted in one of the great adventures in American history.

In perfect secrecy, Clark decided to march on Vincennes in the dead of winter, something the British commander would never have

Old Cahokia Courthouse was built as a residence about 1737. It was sold in 1793 for use as a courthouse and jail. After being displayed in Chicago for many years, it was brought back to Cahokia and reconstructed in 1939. It is thought to be the oldest building in Illinois.

expected would be possible. There were 200 icy, wintry miles (322 kilometers) between Kaskaskia and Vincennes.

In February, with only 170 riflemen, called "Long Knives" because of the deadly long knives they carried, Clark began his march.

A large part of the distance led through flooded river bottoms or swamps. Often they were forced to march through bitter cold water up to their shoulders, holding their guns and powder over their heads to keep them dry. They could not light fires to dry themselves for fear of giving away their presence to unfriendly Indians.

Their success depended entirely on taking the defenders of Vincennes by surprise.

After two weeks, they ran out of food. But although they ate only one meal in five days, they kept on toward Vincennes.

When they reached it at last and stormed the British fort, Hamilton, the British commander, thought he was being attacked by a large force. He could not believe that Clark could have dared to attack with so few men. So Clark captured Vincennes. When the peace treaty was signed after the Revolutionary War, the whole area north of the Ohio River and east of the Mississippi became part of the new United States which was soon to be formed. This was the region known as the *Northwest Territory*.

Without the heroic work of George Rogers Clark and his "Long Knives," it is possible that Illinois and the whole Northwest Territory would not be a part of the United States today. It might very well have remained a part of Canada.

TERRITORIAL DAYS

For their heroic work, each of Clark's men was given 300 acres (121 hectares) of land. Many of them brought their families back to the new land, and other settlers came in. Many of them floated down the Ohio to Shawneetown, Illinois. Others came overland in Conestoga wagons.

Meanwhile, Virginia had given up her claim to Illinois, and Congress had passed an ordinance in 1787 setting up the Northwest Territory. This was one of the most important acts of the new American country.

When the first governor of the Northwest Territory, Arthur St. Clair, visited Kaskaskia in 1783, he created a new county and named it St. Clair, for himself.

In 1800 Illinois became a part of the Indiana Territory; then it 1809 Illinois was made a separate territory with popular Ninian Edwards as its first governor.

Great numbers of settlers began to stream into Illinois, taking more and more of the Indian lands. In 1812 many Indians joined the English in the war against the young United States.

Most of Illinois felt little effect of the War of 1812, but there was a

Ninian Edwards was governor of the Illinois Territory and a United States Senator from Illinois.

23

small settlement around a fort on the shores of Lake Michigan that was in great danger. In 1812, the soldiers were ordered to abandon the fort. One hundred men, women, and children bravely marched out to leave their homes and almost immediately were slaughtered by the Potawatomi Indians.

The little settlement was Chicago, and this was the famous Fort Dearborn Massacre, the worst tragedy in Illinois during the War of 1812.

After the war, so many more settlers began to come in that some Illinois leaders began to think that their territory would soon be ready to become a state.

In order to become a state, a population of forty thousand was needed. It is said that to reach the necessary forty thousand, Illinois counted the travelers and settlers who were only passing through.

Nathaniel Pope, delegate from Illinois in Congress, sponsored a

Chicago, probably about 1779. The insets show Jean Baptiste Point du Sable and his cabin at the mouth of the Chicago River.

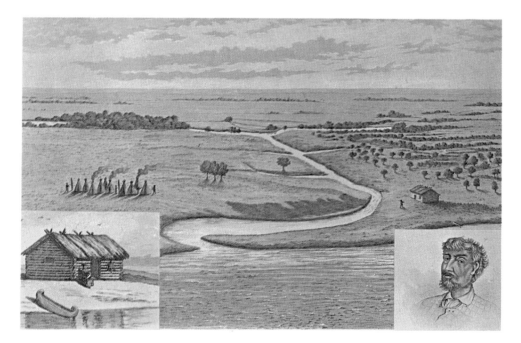

Fort Dearborn was built in 1803 on what is now the south side of the Michigan Avenue Bridge. Bronze plaques now mark the site.

bill to enable Illinois to become a state. His wise action in Congress was responsible for one of the most important events in Illinois history.

Up until this time, the northern boundary of Illinois had been set just to touch the tip of Lake Michigan. Pope argued that the new state should be given a short line on the lake. At his request, the border of the new state was placed 40 miles (64 kilometers) farther north. If this had not been done, Illinois would not have had a lake shoreline. Even more important, it would not have had Chicago and all that Chicago has meant to the state. In the fourteen northern counties added to Illinois by Pope's foresight now live more than half of all of the people of the state.

The act also gave Illinois 2 percent of all money received from the sale of government lands to be used for roads and 3 percent to establish schools.

Illinois became the twenty-first state of the Union on December 3, 1818. Pope wrote home, "We will enter upon a state government with better prospects than any state ever did—the best soil in the world, a mild climate, a large state with the most ample funds to educate every child in the state."

Above: The Indians remaining in Chicago after the
Black Hawk War of 1832 were forced to leave.
This oil painting shows the final meeting of
the Potawatomi on their traditional homesite.
Below: U.S. troops prepare to attack Black Hawk from
their camp in the shadow of the Mississippi bluffs.

Yesterday and Today

LIFE OF A YOUNG STATE

Shadrach Bond became the first governor of the new state. The old town of Kaskaskia was chosen as first capital, and a rented building served as a statehouse. Illinois decided it needed a new town as a capital, so the town of Vandalia was founded in 1819. In 1820 it became the capital, with the understanding that it would remain the capital no longer than twenty years.

By this time, the Indians were rapidly disappearing from Illinois.

In 1829 the government ordered the Sauk and Fox to leave their lands. Three years later, Black Hawk, one of the chiefs, and his followers returned to Illinois, saying the treaty was not legal. They had no plans to make war, but when American soldiers killed two of his men, under a flag of truce, Black Hawk struck back and the Black Hawk War had begun. There were several small battles in this little war that lasted less than three months. Seventy-two settlers were killed and as many as six hundred Indians. Black Hawk was imprisoned for a while. After his release, he went back to his people, and in 1834 Black Hawk died on the Sauk reservation in Iowa at the age of seventy-one.

The Black Hawk War proved to be the last Indian fighting in Illinois. Just one hundred fifty years after Father Marquette first met the Indians in Illinois, they had all been driven out.

Now the last difficulty to the settlement of Illinois was past. The first steamboat, *New Orleans,* had chugged into Shawneetown, Illinois, as early as 1811. Steamboats were bringing settlers in great numbers down the Ohio River from the East. They stopped at Shawneetown, Cairo, or other Illinois river towns. There was even frequent and regular steamboat service on the smaller rivers such as the Illinois as far as Peoria.

At last, it was also possible for goods and settlers to come from the East across the Great Lakes by way of the Erie Canal, which had been completed in 1825. Opening of the canal brought a boom to a tiny village on Lake Michican, called Chicago.

Chicago had been a point to meet and trade since the early days. Marquette was the first European to have a shelter built there. A trader, Jean Baptiste du Sable, from Santo Domingo, had built the first permanent house on the location of Chicago and is considered the city's founder. When du Sable left Chicago, young John Kinzie used the du Sable house for his trading activities. Not many people lived at Chicago when the Dearborn massacre took place.

Twenty-one years later, in 1833, there still were only two hundred people living at Chicago, but they were able to organize a town and give it the name of Chicago. Four years later the city of Chicago was formally incorporated, in 1837, with a population of four thousand.

By this time, other Illinois towns were old and established, with fine homes, churches, and schools and an organized society, while the town that was to become one of the largest in the country was still a sleepy village.

But this sleepy village with its river flowing into the lake proved to be an ideal place to send the trade that was pouring into the Great Lakes from the Erie Canal. The year after Chicago was founded, 225 sailing ships docked there. Also, agricultural products began to arrive in Chicago from the rest of the state to be shipped out to the East by boat. Travelers coming by the water route, with destinations all over the Middle West, left their boats at Chicago; they wanted hotels to stay in and transportation into other parts of the country. Chicago was going to provide all this and more. Chicago was on its way.

Other parts of the state were booming too. Canals were started and railroads planned. The young state was trying to do too much too soon. The depression of 1837 ruined many people and slowed Illinois' progress, but not for long.

The Illinois and Michigan Canal was finished in 1848. The first railroad, the Galena and Chicago Union Railroad, began successful operation in 1848. It was not long before the railroads became more important than the lake, the canals, or the rivers in the growth of Illinois.

In this period of the 1840s, one of the saddest but most unusual series of events of Illinois history took place. Most people would find

The Kinzie house in Chicago in 1832.

it hard to believe that at this time the largest city in Illinois was Nauvoo.

A population of more than twenty thousand had gathered to live at Nauvoo because Joseph Smith, the leader of the Church of Jesus Christ of Latter Day Saints, moved there. Followers of Smith came from all over the country to his new location. These Mormons, as they were called, were forced out of Ohio and moved to Missouri, but they left Missouri to come to Illinois. Misunderstanding of Mormon beliefs and activities often caused their neighbors to turn against them.

Joseph Smith became a powerful leader in Illinois politics. He received a charter for Nauvoo that made him almost independent of the control of the state. He even organized and controlled his own militia. Because he controlled the votes of most of his followers, it might even have been possible for him to influence the results of an election. Some people thought he had plans for becoming president of the United States.

People who were discontented with Smith or disliked his Mormon followers began to spread stories about them. The lie was even told that they were a center for horse thieves. Discontent with Smith and his group grew rapidly, and in 1844 Joseph Smith and his brother were murdered in nearby Carthage. Two years later, the new Mormon leader, Brigham Young, moved on again with almost all of his people, and Nauvoo became a ghost town.

Although thousands once lived in this colorful, religious center, its population today is small. The wonderful Mormon temple disappeared, although it was said to have been the finest building in the country outside of the East. Out of the fine brick homes of thousands of Mormons, only a few remained. Mormon groups now have revived and are restoring Nauvoo as a historic shrine.

A TIME OF TROUBLE

Over the years there had been some people in Illinois who felt strongly that slavery was wrong. But to most Illinoisans the question seemed to have been settled. There were some states where slavery was allowed, and there were others where it was not. According to law, new states coming into the country would not permit slavery.

It was Illinois' own U.S. Senator Stephen A. Douglas who changed all this. His Kansas-Nebraska act made it possible for the people of a territory to decide whether they wanted their region to be slave or

An artist's idea of how the Mormon temple at Nauvoo might have looked if the Mormons had not been driven out. The incomplete temple was destroyed by fire in 1848.

free. Now it was possible that some of the new areas would vote for slavery. Excitement about slavery began to grow again in Illinois.

In 1856, a group of dissatisfied members of many political parties met in Bloomington, Illinois, to form a new party, which they called *Republican*. Both Wisconsin and Michigan also claim to have been the birthplace of the Republican Party, but there are many supporters for Bloomington's claim.

By 1858 the Republicans were able to nominate Abraham Lincoln as their candidate for United States Senator from Illinois. He would try to take the position held by one of the country's most prominent leaders, Senator Douglas of Illinois.

Lincoln challenged Senator Douglas to meet him publicly to debate the issue of slavery. They met seven times before excited crowds, at Ottawa, Freeport, Jonesboro, Charleston, Galesburg, Quincy, and Alton, between August 21 and October 15, 1858.

It was time to decide, Lincoln declared, whether slavery was to grow over free soil or would be confined to its present areas and smothered by time. In his Freeport debate, Lincoln said that because slavery was wrong it must be considered from the moral standpoint. People must decide whether it was right or wrong to hold men and women and children against their will and to oppress them.

Lincoln won the popular vote in this election, but at that time Senators were not elected directly by the vote of the people. The Illinois Legislature had the privilege of choosing the Senator, and the Legislature voted for Douglas.

Although he lost the election, Lincoln had become one of the most famous and well-liked men in America because of the fame of his debates with Senator Douglas. Many Eastern newpapers had carried the debates word for word.

Lincoln was in great demand for speeches in all parts of the country. When he spoke before the Cooper Union Institute in New York, he became even more prominent. More and more people began to speak of him as a possible candidate for president.

The second national convention of the new Republican Party was held in Chicago in May of 1860. The city of Chicago had built a very large new convention hall called the *Wigwam* especially for the

Edward Coles came to Illinois and immediately freed his slaves. It is said he set them free in the middle of the Ohio River, the boundary of freedom.

important event. There Lincoln received his party's nomination for the presidency, although he had decided to remain in Springfield and was not in Chicago at the time of his nomination.

Senator Douglas was nominated by the Democrats to run for the presidency, but his party was split by the slavery trouble. Southern Democrats nominated a candidate of their own to run against both Douglas and Lincoln, and there was also a fourth candidate.

Almost never are two candidates for president chosen from the same state. But here were Illinois' two most famous men running against one another once more, as they had done for most of their lives—this time for the highest office in their nation.

A "COLD WAR" BECOMES A "HOT WAR"

On April 12, 1861, soon after the election of Lincoln, the states of the North and the South were divided by the Civil War. When the

Actors portray Lincoln and Douglas at their Ottawa debate.

war came, many felt that the southern counties of Illinois were more in sympathy with the South than with the North. Stephen A. Douglas was afraid that his state might be divided. He urged all his fellow citizens to put aside their personal feelings and support President Lincoln.

On the day of Lincoln's inauguration, it is said that when Lincoln could not find a place to lay his stovepipe hat to make his speech, Douglas took the hat and held it throughout the speech, as if to say,"Now that the election is over, this is the man who must have our loyalty."

Douglas worked long and hard, and at last was successful. He won over most of the leaders of southern Illinois to the side of the Union. But Douglas had so overworked in his last years that even the strength of the "Little Giant," as he was called, was not enough. He died in June of 1861.

Invasion of southern Illinois was also very likely in the early period of the war. Richard Yates, wartime governor of Illinois, called the Legislature into special session and organized the people for the struggle.

The whole country was unprepared for war, and this was particularly true of Illinois. The army was unorganized, with few guns and supplies. A daring Illinois man, Captain James H. Stokes of

33

Chicago, helped to overcome this early arms shortage. There were supplies at the St. Louis arsenal, but this was surrounded by a howling mob trying to keep the arms from going to Union troops.

Captain Stokes managed to get into the arsenal and remove ten thousand muskets and ammunition to a steamboat that he had arranged to have ready at the dock. When the captain of the boat asked for sailing orders, Stokes said, "Straight to Alton in the regular channel."

"What if we are attacked?" asked the captain. "Then we will fight," replied Stokes.

"But what if we are overpowered?"

"Then run the boat to the deepest water and sink her," Stokes answered.

The boat reached Alton safely, and even the women and children helped to unload the cargo of arms for Illinois soldiers.

Another Illinois hero of the early war was Colonel Elmer Ephraim Ellsworth. He had been a law student in Lincoln's office at Springfield before the war. Colonel Ellsworth led his troops across the Potomac from Washington to capture Alexandria, Virginia, on May 24, 1861. They were successful in driving the Southern troops out. Then Ellsworth spotted a rebel flag flying from a hotel. He ran to the roof, ripped the flag from its mast, and as he was returning to the street, he was shot and killed by the owner of the hotel.

President Lincoln gave Colonel Ellsworth a funeral in the White House. At the funeral the president burst into tears and is supposed to have said, "My boy! My boy! Was it necessary this sacrifice should be made?"

The murder of the young colonel from Illinois became widely known and the words "Remember Ellsworth" served as a rallying cry throughout the North. He was the first man of the Union to die in the Civil War.

With the threat of invasion still hanging over southern Illinois, Governor Yates called on a former army officer and veteran of the Mexican War to defend the Cairo region. This was Ulysses Simpson Grant, who left his home in Galena to accept a new commission as brigadier general in command of the District of Southeastern

34

Missouri, which included southern Illinois. Grant was successful in saving Illinois from becoming a battleground of the Civil War.

From that point on, Grant began the steady rise in influence that made him lieutenant general, then placed him in command of all Union armies in 1864, and finally put him in the White House.

Troops from Illinois played a major part in Grant's campaign to open up the Mississippi River, and Illinois soldiers were on hand in many of the major campaigns of the war—especially at Murfreesboro, with General Sherman at Atlanta, and in his "March to the Sea."

One of the most noted and daring military actions of Illinois regiments in the war was known as "Grierson's Raid." General Benjamin H. Grierson led a Union cavalry troop entirely through the Confederate lines from Tennessee all the way to a meeting with other federal troops in far off Baton Rouge, Louisiana.

Two Illinois men made unusual contributions to winning the war by writing songs that did a great deal to keep up the courage of Northern troops. George F. Root wrote the famous "Tramp, Tramp, Tramp, the Boys Are Marching," "The Battle Cry of Freedom," and "Just Before the Battle, Mother." During the war, possibly the most famous of all the war-time songs was "Marching Through Georgia," written by Henry Clay Work. Both Work and Root were Chicago men.

The effect of such songs is shown by a quotation said to come from a Confederate soldier, "I shall never forget the first time I heard 'Rally Round the Flag.' T'was a nasty night during the 'Seven-days Fight.' I was on picket, when just before taps, some fellow on the other side struck up that song and others joined in the chorus. Tom B. sung out, 'Cap., what are those fellows made of? Here we've licked them six days running, and now on the eve of the seventh they're singing Rally Round the Flag.' I tell you that song sounded to me like the 'knell of doom' and my heart went down into my boots, and it has been an up-hill fight with me ever since that night."

No one knows exactly how many Illinois men served in the Union forces, but one often quoted source puts the figure at 259,092. Only New York, Pennsylvania, and Ohio furnished more troops, but

U.S. Grant portrait by William Cogswell.

these states had much larger populations than Illinois. Illinois lost 34,834 men, including 1,700 who died in Confederate prisons. This was 16.5 percent of the total number of Illinois men in uniform.

Although it was possible to buy one's way out of the draft for three hundred dollars during the Civil War, only fifty-five men in the state avoided military service this way.

A number of Illinois generals besides Grant gained reputations for their success. Major General John A. Logan was one of the best-liked and most respected military leaders. General John M. Palmer, General John Pope, General Stephen A. Hurlbut, General Elon H. Farnsworth, and General Richard Oglesby were others who distinguished themselves.

Illinois' greatest citizen, the commander-in-chief, President Lincoln, was re-elected in 1864. Then only six days after the eventful day when Confederate troops under General Robert E. Lee had surrendered at Appomatox in Virginia, Lincoln was killed by John Wilkes Booth.

One of the most pathetic and memorable events in American history is the long and sad journey of Lincoln's funeral train as it made its way slowly past weeping, mournful crowds all the way home to Illinois, where Lincoln was buried in Springfield, the city he loved.

ILLINOIS GROWS UP

One of the most famous of all veterans' organizations, the Grand Army of the Republic, or GAR, was founded in Illinois at Decatur, April 6, 1866, by an Illinois regimental surgeon, Dr. Benjamin F. Stephenson. The first two national commanders of the GAR were also from Illinois.

Ground was broken for the present Illinois capitol at Springfield in 1868. It was first occupied in 1876, but another twelve years passed before the capitol was fully completed.

Illinois' wartime hero, General U.S. Grant, became president in 1869. Another Illinois wartime hero, General John A. Logan, served for thirteen years in the United States Senate, beginning in 1871.

It may not be true that a cow belonging to a Mrs. O'Leary kicked over a lantern and started the Chicago Fire, but that popular story is told all over the world. Whatever caused it, the Chicago Fire of 1871 was one of the worst disasters ever to hit the state. The flames, carried by a high wind, rushed across the city.

People threw a few belongings into wagons or carried what they could under their arms and dashed in panic through the streets, crowded with their neighbors also trying to escape the fire. Hundreds of people waded into Lake Michigan up to their necks.

The wind carried great sparks through the air, setting fire to the hair and clothing of the fleeing people.

The heat of the fire was so awful that metal coins melted together. Bottles and tumblers and even marbles melted into lumps of glass. Some of the melted lumps and other interesting reminders of the great Chicago Fire can still be seen in the Chicago Historical Society Museum in Lincoln Park.

*On the night of October 8, 1871, the Chicago Fire
started. Several hundred people died and about two hundred
million dollars worth of property was destroyed.*

The fire had covered 3.5 square miles (9 square kilometers) and
left ninety thousand people without homes. Although almost the
entire heart of Chicago was completely destroyed, the people of
Chicago started to build again almost before the burning wreckage
had cooled. Help poured in from all over the country and from all
over the world. Before many years had passed it was not possible to
see traces of the fire at all.

The rebuilding of Chicago after this disaster must be considered one of the great achievements of all time.

In 1886, eight Chicago policemen were killed in a riot at Chicago's Haymarket Square. This unfortunate affair has gone down in history as the "Haymarket Riot." Newspapers everywhere carried the story.

A very much better picture of Chicago was given by the World's Columbian Exposition. The city had won the right to hold this great world's fair in honor of the four hundredth anniversary of the discovery of America by Columbus. The builders of the fair did not quite make it for the anniversary in 1892, but the fair did open the next year.

Probably this was the most beautiful of all the world's fairs ever held, either before or since. If we consider how much more the dollar bought in those days than now, it was also probably the most expensive.

People crowded to Chicago all summer from everywhere in the country and all over the world. They admired the gleaming white buildings, the beautiful calm lagoons. Everything that was new in engineering and agriculture and transportation was shown in exhibits from everywhere in the world.

This was the fair that invented the term *Midway* and this first midway featured thrilling new rides and many other forms of excitement, which some Chicagoans thought was not quite proper.

Over everything on the midway towered the great new ride which had just been invented by Mr. George Washington Gale Ferris. This was a huge wheel on which big passenger cars carried visitors up in the air for a breathtaking view of the fair and of the city. Of course, this was the first Ferris wheel.

Seeing their great fair, most Chicagoans who had never traveled felt that they had come into a wonderful new world for the first time. Although the temporary buildings soon were torn down after the fair, few visitors ever forgot the glimpse of a new kind of beauty that had come into their lives for a while.

At the fair, for the first time, electric lights were used on a grand scale. At night the white buildings shimmered in floodlights. Closely placed lights lined the dome of the administration building and many

*At the Columbian Exposition of 1893 the Ferris wheel,
invented by George Ferris, towered over everything.
Visitors had a spectacular view of the fair and the city
riding this huge wheel, with cars as big as buses.*

AT NIGHT IN THE GRAND COURT

*Electric lights turned the fair into
a brilliant world of color at night.*

others. Colored lights illuminated the fountains and made the night a world of color. For many people who never before had seen even one electric light, this was a wonderful sight.

Some people who came to the fair also wanted to see the remarkable new kind of building that had been springing up in the downtown district of Chicago, called the *Loop*.

When Major William Jenney became the architect for the new Home Insurance Building, he decided to save space and get more light and air by building higher. But until this time the height of buildings had been limited because the higher a building rose into the air the wider its foundations would have to be and the thicker its walls to support the great height. There was bound to be a limit. So Major Jenney worked out a new kind of building, a way to use a skeleton of steel beams to hold up the walls. He became the inventor of what came to be called the skyscraper. This new kind of Chicago building has done more than anything else to change the appearance of the modern city and make its space more usable.

With the "river that flowed backward," Illinois once more captured the attention of the world. Sewage from Chicago had been dumped into the Chicago River. This flowed into Lake Michigan not very far from where the city was pumping out its drinking water. The larger Chicago grew, the more unhealthy its drinking water became.

To change this situation, it was decided to do something that had never been done before.

The Chicago River would be reversed. Instead of flowing to the sea through the Great Lakes and the St. Lawrence River, it would be made to turn backward and flow through the Des Plaines, Illinois, and Mississippi rivers into the Gulf of Mexico, taking the sewage with it.

This required making the Chicago River's South Branch much deeper so that it would flow backward, digging a canal between the Chicago and Des Plaines rivers and installing locks so that boats could travel from one level to another. The plan also required putting locks at the mouth of the Chicago River to keep Lake Michigan from flowing into the river too rapidly.

When this was finished in 1900, it was called the Sanitary and Ship Canal, and authorities have said that it is one of the great engineering projects of all time. The dream of Louis Jolliet of a water route all the way from Lake Michigan to the mouth of the Mississippi had finally come about. Since that time much has been done to treat the sewage, also.

WORLD AT WAR AND WAR IN PEACE

When World War I finally caught up with the United States, our allies needed men, food, and war materials. All of these things Illinois could give, and it is probably true that Illinois did a great deal more than its share in that war.

42

Frank O. Lowden, wartime governor of Illinois, helped to establish the State Council of Defense. This council cooperated with all the wartime groups. Great Lakes Naval Training Station, Camp Grant, and Fort Sheridan were three leading military centers in Illinois. During World War I, 351,153 Illinoisans served in the armed forces.

After the war, Illinois passed into a time sometimes called the *Roaring Twenties*. Chicago and its suburbs became headquarters for gangsters such as Al Capone. Because a number of gangsters were murdered in gang wars, Chicago's reputation suffered throughout the world. Many people in other countries still know Chicago only as the place where the gangster was king.

One of the important events in later Illinois history during the Great Depression was the second world's fair to be held in the state. Chicago's Century of Progress Exposition opened in 1933, just one hundred years after the town had been founded, and so it celebrated Chicago's one hundredth birthday.

Some people thought the buildings were too modern, but most people enjoyed the exhibits, especially the science exhibits where many of the displays were operated by the visitors. The Century of Progress continued in 1934 for another year and was one of the few world's fairs that has ever made a profit.

Another world war began with the bombing of Pearl Harbor on December 7, 1941. Governor Dwight H. Green called a special wartime session of the state legislature and the state prepared to do its part. The Naval Training Station at Great Lakes supplied one-third of all the enlisted personnel in the fleet. Fort Sheridan, Scott Field, and Chanute Field all played an important part in war training. Almost a million men and women from Illinois served in the armed forces during World War II and 27,000 died.

During the war an event happened in Chicago that was to change the world completely. Probably no other single event in all history was ever so important as this one. Yet because it was a military secret only a handful of people knew about it.

The scene of this event was a laboratory underneath the grandstand at the University of Chicago's stadium, called Stagg Field.

Scientists had believed for some time that there was tremendous power in the atom. Of course, the work was very complicated, but the scientists felt after long study that if they could put enough uranium together into one pile and could control the exact amount at all times, they might be able to prove in this test that they could release the power of the atom.

Enrico Fermi, the great Italian scientist, was living in America and was placed in charge of the project in Chicago. He and his associates started out to build what looked like a large brick oven, which they called the "pile." Inside were layers of uranium and graphite.

Many unusual things happened because of the secrecy their work required. Among other things they needed was a large balloon-cloth bag. They asked the Goodyear Rubber Company to make the bag, and the company engineers were greatly puzzled about what anyone would want with a square balloon. When it was finished, the army's new square balloon was the target of much joking.

Meanwhile, the work at Stagg Field continued, and on December 2, 1942, the scientists felt that their uranium pile had about reached the "critical" size; that is, it was ready for testing.

At 8:30 A.M. some of America's most distinguished scientists gathered in what had been the squash court of the stadium. Only forty-two people were on hand to watch history being made. The day went on: the scientists felt they were getting closer and closer. Finally, according to a government report, "Precisely at 3:25 P.M. Chicago time, scientist George Weil withdrew the cadmium-plated control rod and by his action man unleashed and controlled the energy of the atom.

"As those who witnessed the experiment became aware of what had happened, smiles spread over their faces and a quiet ripple of applause could be heard. It was a tribute to Enrico Fermi, Nobel Prize winner, to whom, more than to any other person, the success of the experiment was due."

That night Mrs. Fermi happened to be giving a party for a number of the scientists who had seen the experiment, but she knew nothing about the work that had been done. Later Mrs. Fermi said she could not understand why everybody was complimenting her husband.

Neither she nor anyone else could know that the work of her husband and his fellow scientists had just paved the way for the United States to build the first atomic bomb.

When Dr. Arthur Compton telephoned his report on the experiment to Dr. James B. Conant, he said in code, "The Italian navigator [Fermi] has landed in the New World."

"How were the natives?" asked Conant.

"Very friendly."

The scientists who first took power from the atom on the squash court at the University of Chicago must have hoped that the atom could be used for peaceful purposes as well as for atom bombs. Dr. Fermi was dead, but others of the group surely were pleased when nuclear power from the atom was used in 1960 to generate electricity at the Dresden, Illinois, power plant. This was the largest all-nuclear power plant in North America.

Another great event took place a considerable distance from Illinois, but it is usually considered to be one of the great events of modern times, especially as Illinois' future is concerned.

Ever since the time of Marquette and Jolliet, boats had been stopping at Chicago. However, the larger ocean freighters could never travel between the ocean and the Great Lakes because the waterway up the St. Lawrence River was not deep enough and the locks were too small.

Men had dreamed of widening and deepening this waterway almost from the beginning, but the work was not finished until 1959 when the wonderful new St. Lawrence Seaway was completed as a project of the United States and Canada working together.

For the first time, Chicago and other Illinois ports were really opened to the ocean shipping of the whole world. More than half the world's ships are able to travel the St. Lawrence Seaway to Chicago's Calumet "seaport."

During the 1960s the gift of a Picasso sculpture to the city provided its world-famous artistic symbol. Not so happy were the events of the Democratic National Convention at Chicago in 1968. Rioters tried in every way possible to break up the convention, and they claimed police brutality, which later proved to be much exaggerated.

The John Hancock Building and the Water Tower Place as seen from the Fourth Presbyterian Church.

Illinois adopted a new state constitution the first year of the 1970s. The National Accelerator Laboratory opened at Batavia in 1971, and in 1973 the Sears building in Chicago became the tallest building in the world.

After leading his city for twenty-one years, Mayor Richard J. Daley of Chicago died unexpectedly on December 20, 1976. His iron control and firm but benevolent grip on the city's government had given him a worldwide reputation, as well as the name of "king maker" on the U.S. political scene.

THE PEOPLE OF ILLINOIS

Illinois was French before it was American, and a few descendants of these first settlers may still be found. Early American settlement of Illinois was mostly of native stock, particularly from the South. As the waves of immigration from Europe increased, Illinois proved particularly attractive, both on the farms and in the cities, and it still is.

By the twentieth century, Chicago counted more Dutch, Scandinavians, Poles, Lithuanians, Bohemians, Croations, and Greeks than any other city in the United States.

Few other large cities have such a wide ethnic mixture. Smaller communities were founded by different ethnic groups or have been dominated by one group at some time.

Wherever the newcomers came from or wherever they went, they found life hard at first, but eventually gained increasing success and acceptance.

The "melting pot" process continues, with large numbers of Mexicans, Pakistanis, Indians, Germans, Poles, Italians, Cubans, Russians, and others finding a home in Illinois. Chicago claims to have the largest Greek community anywhere and Chicago has also become home to a large number of Puerto Ricans.

Blacks have contributed to Illinois life since Jean Baptiste Point du Sable founded Chicago in 1779. He was said to have "a fine establishment in the midst of a wilderness . . . a man of substance."

The black population in Illinois was small, but they were able to make some progress in government and civil rights. John W.E. Thomas of Chicago became the first black elected as a state representative. In 1885 the Illinois General Assembly passed a civil rights act forbidding racial discrimination in restaurants, hotels, theaters, railroads, streetcars, and places of public accommodation and amusement.

Governmental history was made in 1929 when Oscar De Priest of Chicago was seated in the United States House of Representatives. He was the first black Congressman ever seated from the North. In 1934 Arthur W. Mitchell of Chicago became the first black of the Democratic Party in Congress.

Black population in Illinois increased dramatically during and after World Wars I and II. This brought many new problems as well as opportunities.

Despite many gains, throughout the 1960s and 1970s many problems have remained for the blacks of Illinois: fair treatment in the purchase of real estate, quality education, and equal opportunities for employment and advancement.

As the 1970s drew to a close, all of the people of Illinois were aware of both problems and opportunities.

*A few small areas of prairie land remain just as they
were when the first Europeans saw them. Conservationists
have been trying very hard to preserve these, and it
appears that some will be saved. However, others are
restoring small areas, as in the Prairie Restoration
Project of the Morton Arboretum pictured above at Lisle.*

48

Natural Treasures

TREASURES UNDER THE GROUND

When the glaciers finally melted from Illinois, they left, over most of the state, a layer of fertile soil sometimes as deep as 100 feet (30 meters). This fine soil of Illinois is usually considered to be the single greatest natural treasure of the state.

,There is more soft coal under the surface of Illinois than any other state. As much as two thirds of all Illinois has coal lying under it. Even after the many years coal has been taken from Illinois, it is estimated that there are still billions of tons of coal remaining.

Peat is also found in the swamps and lakes of northeast Illinois.

Oil and gas are valuable mineral treasures. Experts have estimated that nearly 200 million barrels (172,200,000 metric tons) of oil and 400 billion cubic feet (12 billion cubic meters) of gas can still be removed from under the surface of oil lands in the state. These reserves are located in the south and central parts of the state.

Other minerals found in Illinois have been important in the development of the state. Limestone is found in large deposits along the Mississippi River and in other areas. Sand and gravel are also plentiful in Illinois, in the northern section. One of the largest deposits of silica sand in the world is found near Ottawa. Clay comes from thirty-three counties in Illinois. Fluorspar, lead, zinc, and tripoli are important. Although gypsum, anhydrite, barite, pyrite, and feldspar sands are found in Illinois, they are not much used at present. Salt springs and salt brine are found in large quantities.

LIVING TREASURES

When Illinois first was settled about 40 percent of the state was covered with trees. Today only about 10 percent of Illinois is forested, covering about 4,000,000 acres (1,600,000 hectares). Oak, hickory, mixed hardwoods, white oak, and scrub hardwoods are the most important types of trees.

There is a good growth of forest crop in Illinois, with several hundred million board feet growing annually. This is considerably more than is used in a year, so Illinois' supply of trees for lumber and other uses is growing every year.

Most of the forest lands are found along the rivers in the higher lands. Much of the forest land that was cleared for crops was not very good for agriculture and a large part of it is now being placed back into forest.

In addition to trees, Illinois soil and climate combine to grow 2,400 other kinds of plants.

About three hundred kinds of birds regularly nest in Illinois. Each fall as many as a million ducks migrate to the south over the route known as the Mississippi Flyway, which makes the state one of the great duck hunting areas. Bobwhite quail and ringneck pheasant are two other important game birds in Illinois

Fifty kinds of mammals are native to Illinois. Muskrats, minks, and raccoons are the main fur-bearing animals. Deer, rabbits, and squirrels are also plentiful.

There are 180 species of fish living in Illinois rivers and lakes.

The People Use Their Treasures

WEALTH FROM THE SOIL

At one time almost everyone living in Illinois had to grow crops to provide enough food. Now only about 5 percent of all the people in Illinois make their living by farming, and this small number provides more than enough for all the needs of all the people.

Agricultural machines have come into general use. Now one man with machines can do the work of many laboring by hand. New seeds and new kinds of crops such as hybrid corn, the use of fertilizers for the soil—all have made it possible for each acre of farmland to grow a great deal more than it once did.

Corn is still the most important single crop in Illinois. The state ranks first or second every year in the production of corn.

A large percentage of all the soybeans produced in the United States is grown in Illinois. Hay, alfalfa, clover, apples, peaches, and melons are other important crops. Illinois ranks fourth in total agriculture behind California, Iowa, and Texas.

Decatur is a leading soybean processing center, and Belleville is the center of a rather unusual activity—the growing of bleached asparagus.

Because of the enormous amount of grain grown in Illinois and the surrounding states and because of the rail and boat transportation coming into the city, Chicago has become one of the world's leading grain markets.

The small town of Pana is a marketing center of another kind. Sixty acres (24 hectares) of greenhouses near Pana grow nothing but roses. Twenty million cut roses each year go out from Pana to the flower lovers of the country.

WEALTH FROM LIVING THINGS

Illinois farmers grow more hogs than any other state except Iowa. The state also ranks high in beef, dairy cattle, and poultry.

An early lithograph of an Illinois farm.

Most people are surprised by the size of the fishing industry in Illinois. Each year commericial fishermen take several hundred million dollars worth of fish from rivers and lakes in Illinois. Two thirds of all this catch comes from the Mississippi and Illinois rivers, the rest from Lake Michigan. Carp, buffalo fish, sheepshead, channel cat, flathead cat, blue cat, and bullheads are the main commercial fish.

At one time, lake trout were an important part of the catch, but Lake Michigan was invaded by lamprey eels from the ocean. These eels attach themselves to lake trout and kill them. Most of the trout in the Great Lakes were killed by the lamprey. But efforts to control the lamprey succeeded, and lake trout fishing may become important again in Illinois. Salmon have been introduced to Lake Michigan and are caught in large numbers.

When the early explorer La Salle came to Illinois, his main interest was the fur animals in Illinois. Even today, muskrats, raccoons, and minks are trapped for their furs in Illinois.

UP OUT OF THE GROUND

Probably the first use of minerals in Illinois history was that of salt. Prehistoric Indians in Illinois undoubtedly used the salt springs to produce the salt they needed. When the Europeans came, brines from the salt springs of Gallatin County became the basis of a thriving salt industry. Salt water was poured into evaporating basins, and the salt was scraped into containers after the water had dried. As much as 300,000 bushels (10,570,000 liters) of salt per year were produced this way in the area around Equality.

Producing salt for table use became unprofitable in Illinois, but now salt water is used in Illinois in a way the early people could never have imagined. Almost half of the oil produced in Illinois depends on the use of salt brine. This brine is pumped into the oil bearing rocks to force out the oil. Later, it is hoped that salt brined in Illinois will find many other uses in the production of chemicals.

Lead mining was also one of the earliest activities in Illinois. Before 1850, lead mining had made Galena the largest and most important city in the state. It was the metropolis and Chicago was a small trading center. Then lead mining became generally unprofitable in the area about the mid-1800s. Visitors to Galena can still see the remains of many of the old lead mines all around the area.

Coal mining is not as important in Illinois as it once was, but the state still ranks fourth in coal production. If a way can be found to make Illinois coal burn "cleaner," there may be a vast increase in production for the nation's energy needs.

At present a large part of the coal is mined by what is called strip mining, where the top soil layer is taken off, the coal exposed to the surface, and then stripped away by great machines.

Oil has been adding to Illinois' wealth since 1883.

Natural gas production in Illinois amounts to several billion cubic feet per year, but this is only a small part of the natural gas used by the state, and gas is brought in from outside. The largest underground storage field in the country for natural gas is at Herscher. This field can hold more natural gas than Illinois produces in a year.

Although limestone is a widely used building material, limestone

Galena at the height of its mining boom in the nineteenth century.

has far more uses for industry than for building. This important mineral is used for road building, concrete making, fertilizer, railroad ballast, and metal processes, among others. Products made of Illinois clay include brick, pottery, white ware, sewer pipe, and many other important products.

Illinois leads the nation in the production of fluorspar. This mineral is the base of fluorine, which is employed in many ways in the chemical industry and now finds a critical use in rocket fuels.

TURNING RAW MATERIALS INTO WEALTH

The Chicago area is the largest manufacturing center in the United States. About three-fourths of all the factories in Illinois are in Cook County, but other important factories are located throughout the state.

Illinois is first in the production of farm machinery and electrical merchandise.

The Moline-Rock Island area is known as the "Farm Machinery Capital of the World." The John Deere Company has manufactured farm implements there ever since Mr. Deere moved his factory to

Moline in 1848. International Harvester Company, Minneapolis-Moline Implement Company, J.I. Case, and many smaller concerns all manufacture farm implements in the area.

Illinois ranks high among the states in the manufacture of bricks and furniture. The largest plant in the United States for making bottles and other glass containers is at Alton.

Chicago is no longer "Hog Butcher to the World," as Carl Sandburg, the poet, once called it, but as a whole, the state is still one of the leaders in meat packing.

Chicago, however, continues to be a leader in many industries, such as in the manufacture of diesel engines, pumps, conveyor equipment, food machinery, valves, electronic products, paper boxes, and telephone equipment. The Chicago area is also a leader in steel products. One out of every four candy bars made in the United States is a product of Chicago. The city is home to the largest mail order firms in the world.

The largest broom factory in the world operates at Paris, Illinois. To feed this factory, the region around Mattoon grows a crop not very familiar to most people. The area is a leading producer of broom corn.

THE CROSSROADS OF NORTH AMERICA

Someone has said that "Illinois is the center of all the travel in the United States. If people or goods are moving anywhere in the U.S. it is likely that they will go through Illinois."

Possibly Chicago's best claim to fame is that of the world's greatest railroad and air-transport center. More trains and railroads operate through and around Chicago than anywhere else. For the size of the state, Illinois' railroad mileage is the greatest in the country, and only Texas, with its much larger area, has more actual miles of rails.

Chicago's Midway Airport was once the busiest in the world, but it lost its title with the coming of the commercial jet planes. Now Chicago's O'Hare International Airport has taken the title and han-

55

Unit District #5 Elementary
Instructional Media Center

Chicago is a leader in the production of steel. Reinforcing bars and post tensioning were used by Inland Steel in constructing a nuclear power plant project near Rockford. The building was constructed in the late 1970s.

56

These two terminal buildings at O'Hare Airport serve mostly domestic flights.

dles more commericial flights daily than any other airport.

Illinois is also still one of the great centers of water transportation, with 581 miles (935 kilometers) of Mississippi River frontage, 113 miles (182 kilometers) of Ohio River frontage and 330 miles (531 kilometers) of the Illinois waterway, in addition to the Lake Michigan frontage, which makes Chicago the greatest port on the Great Lakes. Some experts predict that as the traffic grows on the St. Lawrence Seaway Chicago could become one of the leading ports of the world.

East St. Louis, Illinois, is also a leading transportation center. Pipelines for carrying crude oil, natural gas, and refined products stretch for thousands of miles over Illinois. These lines also carry most of the oil which has to be brought into Illinois from outside the state.

GETTING THE MESSAGE ACROSS

The first newspaper in Illinois was the *Herald*, first published in 1814 at Kaskaskia. Today, Chicago's newspapers are among the best-known in the country.

Chicago is one of the world's largest printing centers. More encyclopedias, catalogs, and maps are produced there than anywhere else. Chicago is also a leading center in the publishing of textbooks and educational and industrial tests.

The first "dramatic production" ever televised was sent out by the experimental television station W9XAP of Chicago in 1931.

Human Treasures

THE RAIL SPLITTER

More words have been written about Abraham Lincoln than about any other American. Lincoln was not born in Illinois, and his worldwide fame came after he had left Illinois. But Lincoln did consider Illinois his home, and it was in Illinois that his greatness was shaped and molded.

Lincoln was born in Hardin County, Kentucky, February 12, 1809. The family moved to Illinois when Abraham was a grown man of twenty-one. In 1831 Lincoln and his two stepbrothers helped to build a flatboat and pilot its load of produce down the Mississippi River as far as New Orleans.

On the way down the Sangamon River at New Salem, their flatboat stuck on the mill dam, where the bow turned up toward the sky and water began to flow in. People looking on gave a number of suggestions about getting the boat free. But Lincoln took off some of the cargo and borrowed an augur. After he drilled a hole in the bow and let the water out, he filled the hole with a plug, and they were able to float the boat off the dam.

The things Lincoln saw and his experiences on this trip are not very well known, but they must have given this brilliant young man a new idea of what life could be like beyond the rough, pioneer country which was all he had known before.

After his trip down the river, Lincoln returned to Illinois, where he settled at New Salem. There he was a laborer (probably splitting rails for fences to earn his name "rail splitter"), a storekeeper, postmaster, surveyor, soldier, and legislator—and began his study of law.

The years at New Salem are generally considered to be the turning point of his life.

Lincoln often joked about his service in the Black Hawk War in 1832. His last enlistment in that war was under the unlikely leader-

Opposite: Abe Lincoln, the rail splitter.

ship of a minister, the Reverend Jacob M. Early, who was also a doctor. The last two weeks of their enlistment they searched through the swamps for Black Hawk but never found him.

When he spoke about the leadership of General Lewis Cass in the war, Lincoln poked fun at the General. "If General Cass went in advance of me picking huckleberries, I guess I surpassed him in charges upon the wild onions.

"If he saw any live, fighting Indians it was more than I did; but I had a good many bloody struggles with the mosquitoes, and I can truly say I was often hungry."

Defeated for the state Legislature in 1832, Lincoln tried again in 1834 and won. One of his first important activities in government was his success in getting the state capital moved to Springfield. He did this with a group of eight other members of the Legislature who were called the "Long Nine" because they were so tall. The total height of these nine lawmakers was 54 feet (16.4 meters).

Lincoln did not begin to practice law until 1837, when he moved from New Salem to Springfield. There he married Mary Todd, and the first of their four sons, Robert Todd Lincoln, was born in 1843.

Three years later Lincoln was elected to the House of Representatives for his first and only term in the U.S. Congress. This backwoods lawyer was admitted to practice law before the Supreme Court of the United States in 1849, but he lost the only case he took before the Supreme Court, Lewis vs. Lewis.

Growing more prominent, he was offered the post of secretary of the Oregon Territory and later the position of governor of the Oregon Territory, but refused both appointments.

One of the saddest days for the Lincolns came in 1850 when their second son, Edward Baker Lincoln, died after being "sick for fifty-two days." Many writers have said that Mr. Lincoln never quite recovered from Edward's death.

In that same year William Wallace Lincoln, their third son, was born.

Lincoln's reputation and success as a lawyer grew in this period. His wonderful stories and good humor made people fond of his company. His bids to become a United States Senator from Illinois were

60

defeated both in 1854 and 1858. After the defeat in 1858, he wrote to an unhappy friend, "Quit that. You will soon feel better. Another 'blow up' is coming; and we shall have fun again."

It was this "fun" that elected him to the presidency in 1860.

Not until he was elected president did Lincoln change his appearance with one of the most familiar features that we know today. A young girl, eleven-year-old Grace Bedell of Westfield, New York, had written to him suggesting that he would look better if he wore a beard. Lincoln replied, "As to the whiskers, having never worn any, do you not think people would call it a piece of silly affectation if I were to begin it now?" But when he took the oath of office, he became not only the first Republican president, but also the first president of the United States to wear a beard.

Many sadnesses came to the Lincolns during his life as president: defeat in battles, the bitter words of people who did not like his actions, and the treachery of several friends and associates.

Among the worst of these blows was the death in the White House in 1862 of William Wallace Lincoln, just eleven years old. It is thought that Mrs. Lincoln never fully recovered from William's death and the illness of his younger brother, Thomas (Tad) Lincoln, who had been born in 1853.

The remainder of the Lincolns' story is known to everyone. "The gaunt figure of one man stands above all the rest. The prairie son gave his life so that 'government of the people, by the people, for the people, shall not perish from the earth.' The bullet which silenced his words could not silence the spirit of them—'with malice toward none; with charity for all.' "

And so the great man came home to Springfield, where his body was laid to rest in Oak Ridge Cemetery.

Those who heard Lincoln's "farewell address" to the people of Springfield at the railroad station as he left for Washington to become president said later that he appeared to know he would never return alive to the home in Springfield he loved so much.

Although he was born and grew up a poor boy, Lincoln was successful in his law practice. When he died, he left a net estate of $110,296.80, not including his real estate.

In 1870 Congress gave Mrs. Lincoln an annual pension of the small sum of $3,000. Just before she died in Springfield in 1882, Congress increased the pension to five thousand dollars plus a gift of fifteen thousand dollars.

"Tad" Lincoln died in 1871, but the Lincolns' oldest son, Robert Todd Lincoln, lived until 1926. Robert Lincoln served as United States minister to Britain and as secretary of war.

A SOLDIER-PRESIDENT

Ulysses S. Grant left his home in Galena, Illinois, to go to the Civil War, and he came back to Galena after the war, but Grant had been born in Ohio and lived most of his life outside of Illinois. Although he had tried many types of work he had not been successful. Finally he went to work for his father, who owned a leather-goods store in Galena.

Grant's home is now a Galena shrine.

As the Civil War went on, Grant became more and more prominent. He won a great victory after the long siege of Vicksburg. President Lincoln appointed him commander-in-chief of the armies. On April 9, 1865, the famous surrender of General Lee took place at Appomattox, and General Grant was praised for his generous treatment of the conquered Southern army. He even permitted the Southern men to take their horses with them because they would be needed for spring plowing.

In 1869, Grant responded once more to his country's call and became the 18th president of the United States. Everyone respected the president for his honesty, but he had a difficult time as president. Once more he returned to Galena. He had financial troubles and as his life drew to a close it appeared that his country had forgotten him. If it had not been for the strange and complicated story of James Wilson, the Congressman from Iowa, who gave up his seat in Congress so that Grant would have a government pension, the great man from Galena might have died without any further recognition from his country during his lifetime.

THE LITTLE GIANT

He was only 5 feet 4 inches tall (162.6 centimeters) but his size could not keep him from becoming a "giant" in politics, and so they nicknamed Stephen A. Douglas the "Little Giant."

Like Lincoln, Douglas had come to Illinois as a young man of twenty-one, taking a job as a teacher and studying law. Six years later he had been state's attorney for the first Judicial Circuit, a state legislator, register of the federal land office at Springfield, secretary of state of Illinois, and a justice of the state supreme court, the youngest supreme court judge in the history of the state—all before the age of twenty-eight.

When Douglas ran as the Democratic candidate for Congress in 1837, his opponents laughed, but Douglas campaigned so hard he lost by only thirty-five votes! Running again in 1843, he won the election, and four years later was elected Senator. He served in Congress during one of the most critical periods in United States history.

His greatest ambition was to become president. His friends tried to get the Democratic nomination for him in 1852, but many people felt that at thirty-nine he was too young. In 1856 he lost out to Buchanan. When he won the Senate seat over Abraham Lincoln in 1858, it was certain that he would become the Democratic candidate in 1860, but by that time it was too late. Douglas had angered the Democrats of the South; they split away from the party and Douglas lost the election.

At the beginning of the Civil War, Douglas saw clearly that the United States must be preserved. He toured the old Northwest Territory, rallying undecided people to support Lincoln and the federal government. Possibly he did more than any one individual to keep many parts of the country from siding with the South.

But Stephen Douglas had broken his health in the election and in his tiring speeches for the Union. He died in 1861, and his last message was, "Tell my children to live and uphold the Constitution."

MEN TO GOVERN ILLINOIS

Handsome and popular Shadrach Bond was Illinois' first governor. In the early days of Illinois the governors had little real power. However, the second governor, Edward Coles, led and won the fight to keep slavery from Illinois. When he came to Illinois, Coles freed his own slaves in a dramatic ceremony in a boat in the middle of the Ohio River.

No governor of Illinois has become president, but Adlai E. Stevenson, the 31st governor of Illinois, was twice Democratic candidate for president, running against Dwight D. Eisenhower. Mr. Stevenson later became United States ambassador to the United Nations. The first Adlai E. Stevenson, a grandfather of Governor Stevenson, was also prominent in Illinois politics and served as vice-president of the United States under Grover Cleveland.

Other family names appear more than once in Illinois politics.

64

Richard Yates was the state's Civil War governor from 1861 to 1865. His son, Richard Yates, Jr., was governor from 1901 to 1905.

The only man in Illinois history to be elected governor three times was Richard J. Oglesby, who succeeded the first Yates as governor. Oglesby's terms were scattered. After his first term, he was followed by John M. Palmer. Then in 1873 Palmer was succeeded by Oglesby. Ten days after he took office, Oglesby resigned to become a United States Senator. Twelve years later, in 1885, Richard Oglesby again became governor of Illinois.

When John P. Altgeld was elected, he became the first Democratic governor of Illinois in thirty-six years. He is probably best remembered for pardoning three of the men who had been convicted of the murder of Chicago policemen during the Haymarket Riot. Altgeld thought these men had been convicted unjustly, but he was not reelected for another term as governor. Recent prominent political figures include Senators Charles Percy and Adlai E. Stevenson, III, Mayors Richard J. Daley and Michael Bilandic of Chicago, and Governor James Thompson.

SUCH INTERESTING PEOPLE

Men and women of Illinois have gained fame in almost every field. One of the reasons for Chicago's rapid growth was the drive and ability of the men who were the early leaders.

The name of Potter Palmer became known everywhere for developing State Street into the leading business street of the city. For many years Mrs. Potter Palmer was the leader of society in Chicago, and it was said she "ruled like a queen." Marshall Field built his department store into one of the greatest stores in the world. His descendants, also named Marshall Field, entered the publishing business.

Another of Illinois' great merchants was A. Montgomery Ward, who founded the great mail order company still bearing his name.

John Deere, of farm machinery fame; Cyrus H. McCormick, inventor of the reaper; George Pullman, with his Pullman railroad

Some of the men who were important to the history of
Illinois. Above left: William Butler Ogden, the first mayor
of Chicago. Above right: Nathaniel Pope, Illinois'
territorial delegate in Congress. Below, left to right:
Me-No-Quet, a Potawatomi chief; Black Hawk, a Sauk
and Fox chief; and Wa-Baun-See, a Potawatomi chief.

Father Jacques Marquette, painted by Dr. Harry Wood of Arizona State University after much historical research.

sleeping car; and Joseph Glidden, who invented barbed wire, can be listed as a few among the many Illinois men who have helped to change our way of life with their inventions and new industries.

One of the most famous Illinois names is that of Jane Addams. Due to her ever-continuing effort, Hull House became probably the most famous settlement house anywhere. Jane Addams received the Nobel Prize and when she died she was given recognition from every part of the globe as the greatest woman of her times.

At one time the Chicago area was considered headquarters for the greatest writers in the country. The famous poet Carl Sandburg gained much of his fame in Chicago and wrote a noted poem about the city. Ernest Hemingway, of Oak Park, won the Nobel Prize for literature.

The musician and conductor, Theodore Thomas, was joked about in the East when he planned to bring his symphony orchestra to play for the uncultured people of Chicago, but Dr. Thomas liked the people of the Midwest, who responded to fine music. He founded the Chicago Symphony, and before long in Chicago he had developed one of the finest symphonies anywhere. This record was kept and improved by his successor, Frederick Stock. Recent conductors of international fame have added to this reputation, until the Chicago Symphony now is called by many authorities the finest in the world.

An unusual personality who called Illinois home was William Ashley Sunday. "Billy" Sunday was a professional baseball player with Pop Anson's old Chicago White Stockings. Disgusted with the life he was living, Sunday resigned from baseball and became a worker in the YMCA of Chicago. Then he became an evangelist. Dramatic methods in the pulpit came naturally to him. He leaped over the pulpit as easily as he had leaped for a high fly. He might roll on the floor or tear his hair, but his sermons had such sincere warmth and message that thousands were converted.

Another athlete who was tempted to quit athletics to become a minister was Amos Alonzo Stagg. Amos Stagg decided that he could be a greater influence for good by remaining a football coach. He continued to coach until he was past ninety. During the more than

68

one hundred years of his life, Coach Stagg became one of the best-known and best-loved figures in the country.

In addition to duSable, Illinois has produced many notable blacks. Dr. Daniel Hale Williams performed the first successful heart operation. John Hope Franklin was a distinguished black scholar and chairman of the history department at the University of Chicago.

Outstanding black personalities have gained world reputations. Some of these include renowned singer Mahalia Jackson; Pulitzer Prize winning poet, playwright, and poet laureate of Illinois Gwendolyn Brooks; distinguished scientist Percy Julian; John Johnson, founder and developer of one of the country's leading publishing operations; Archibald Carey, distinguished attorney and alternate delegate to the United Nations; Dr. Theodore K. Lawless; Judge James B. Parson; and Chicago Cubs' baseball star, Ernie Banks, long known as "Mr. Cub," to list only a few.

The Quadrangle at the University of Illinois Champaign-Urbana campus. The domed building is the auditorium building.

70

Teaching and Learning

When Illinois first became a state, 3 percent of all the money coming from the sale of state land was set aside for education. This respect for education has had its effect ever since.

The first institution of higher education in Illinois was Illinois College at Jacksonville, founded in 1829.

The University of Illinois, now with one of the largest enrollments in the world, was founded as Illinois Industrial University in 1862. The university introduced the first state-supported school of music in the United States. It was the first school to offer architectural education west of the Allegheny Mountains and the first betatron apparatus in the world was completed at the University of Illinois in 1940, for research on the atom.

In addition to the campus at Urbana, the University of Illinois has a large Chicago campus, and a famous medical school in Chicago. The medical campus includes the schools of pharmacy, dentistry, and nursing as well as medicine.

Southern Illinois University, several statewide institutions, and some Chicago-area schools are supported by the state.

Some of the best-known private colleges are found in Illinois.

The University of Chicago is known to do things differently. The university chose in 1929 as its president the youngest president of a great university, Robert Maynard Hutchins. Dr. Hutchins is often said to have turned the world of education upside down. Under Dr. Hutchins' direction, the University of Chicago tried such new ideas as letting students enter the college, whether they had finished high school or not, if they could pass the entrance tests—no matter what their age. The latest president is Hanna Holborn Gray.

Other well-known Illinois colleges and universities are Northwestern University and National College of Education, both at Evanston; Monmouth College, Monmouth; Illinois Wesleyan, Bloomington; Loyola University, Roosevelt University, Mundelein College, Illinois Institute of Techology, and De Paul University, Chicago; and Blackburn at Carlinville.

Illinois' first school law was not passed until 1825, when school

The University of Chicago.

districts were provided for, along with a compulsory tax to finance an education for children, but the taxation clause was removed in 1829, and there were few public schools in Illinois. Chicago's first public school opened in 1841.

Until 1856 high school education was provided by a few private academies. In that year, Chicago High School became one of the first public high schools to be established west of the Alleghenies. It later was renamed Central High School and finally discontinued.

Today, of course, a large part of the budgets of both the state and local areas is devoted to public education. In fact, education is the most costly item of public expenditure.

In addition to public schools, there are many well-known private schools and large numbers of parochial schools. Among private schools with a national reputation may be listed the North Shore Country Day School at Winnetka, Latin and Francis Parker schools in Chicago, and many such specialized schools as the School of the Art Institute of Chicago, said to be the largest of its kind anywhere.

Among the several religious denominations that maintain schools, the Roman Catholic school system is by far the largest.

72

Enchantment of Illinois

LAND OF LINCOLN

The number and variety of places set aside, restored, or preserved to the memory of Abraham Lincoln and his family in Illinois makes the "Lincoln Country" outstanding. Probably nowhere else is there such a complete coverage of the life of any other man in the way of the places and things associated with his life.

Visitors in autos today can whiz over almost the same route that was so long and difficult for the Lincoln family as they came into Illinois from Indiana. This route is now well marked as the "Lincoln National Memorial Highway." There were no highways then as the oxen pulled loaded wagons over frozen mud and forded chilly streams.

A bronze statue of youthful Abraham Lincoln marks the beginning of this Memorial Highway near Lawrenceville. It shows Lincoln walking beside the family's covered wagon.

Fifteen days after they left Indiana, the Thomas Lincoln family settled on government land on the Sangamon River southwest of Decatur. The place is now maintained as Lincoln Trail Homestead Park. A large boulder marks the location of the family cabin.

After a year at the first Illinois home, Lincoln's father and step-mother settled near Charleston, which is now Lincoln Log Cabin State Park. Lincoln did not move with his family to this house, but his parents spent their remaining years there.

Near this cabin is the Moore Home State Memorial, where Lincoln ate a last meal with his stepmother before leaving for his inauguration in Washington. Lincoln's father and stepmother are buried in the Thomas Lincoln Cemetery, renamed for the senior Lincoln in 1935.

The only memorial of its kind is the great work that has been done at New Salem, Illinois, to restore a complete town just as it was in Lincoln's day, in memory of the great man.

Here Lincoln lived for six years, and those six years were almost the entire life of the town, strange as that seems. New Salem had

Visitors recapture memories of Abraham Lincoln when they explore the restored New Salem buildings.

been founded with the hope that it would become prosperous with river traffic on the Sangamon River.

Lincoln himself was one of the pilots for a steamboat named *The Talisman,* which came up the river loaded with goods and arrived at Portland Landing. On the return trip they had to tear down part of the dam at New Salem to let the boat pass. So it was clear that this part of the Sangamon was not deep enough for steamboats.

The little town of New Salem never had more than one hundred inhabitants. It lived for only ten years and became a ghost town. Only one of the original buildings is still standing. This is the Onstot cooperage shop, built in 1834. Other buildings now seen at New Salem have been carefully rebuilt. These include thirteen cabins, six shops, and the Rutledge Tavern.

Buildings at New Salem have been furnished as nearly as possible as they were when Lincoln lived there. A post office is operated in the Lincoln-Berry store building where Lincoln served as postmaster.

Visitors to the New Salem State Park enjoy riding about the park in a covered wagon pulled by oxen. A museum in the park features items in use in the period when Lincoln called New Salem home. More than a million people visit New Salem each year to see the scenes of Lincoln's bachelor days.

Not far from New Salem and only 23 miles (37 kilometers) northeast of Springfield is the town of Lincoln, Illinois. This is the only town named for Lincoln while he was still living. There is a very interesting story about how the town of Lincoln received its name.

Lincoln was the lawyer for the founders of the town, who decided to give their new project the name of their lawyer. Lincoln protested, saying, "I never knew anything named Lincoln that amounted to anything." However, he finally agreed, and after the town site had been laid out, a crowd gathered to dedicate it, with Abraham Lincoln as master of ceremonies.

In his hand he took a large watermelon, which he neatly cut open with his pocket knife and split in two on the wagon where he was standing. Taking out the core, Lincoln squeezed the watermelon juice into a tin cup.

"I now christen this town site. Its name is Lincoln!" he proclaimed and poured the watermelon juice on the ground in humorous dedication.

Then he continued, "I have also prepared a feast for this occasion." He pulled a covering off a wagon load of watermelons, and the crowd did have a feast, indeed. Now the town of Lincoln attracts a large number of visitors in honor of its dedication by Abraham Lincoln, whose name it bears.

Probably there are more Lincoln memories in Springfield than anywhere else in Illinois. There, at 8th and Jackson, is the only house Lincoln ever owned. It had been a story and a half in height, but Mrs. Lincoln had it remodeled into two stories while Lincoln was away from home. She is supposed to have used money received from her father. Lincoln purchased the home for $1,500 in 1844, and the Lincoln son, Robert Todd Lincoln, presented it to the state as a shrine in 1887.

Made of native hardwoods, the house has framework and floors of oak with laths of hand-split hickory. The original shingles were hand-split walnut. Wooden pegs and handmade nails were used in its construction. Today it is painted Quaker brown, as it was when the Lincolns lived there. Some of the original Lincoln furnishings can be seen in the house. Other furnishings have been collected as nearly like the originals as possible.

The former capitol building of Illinois, the one used just before the present capitol building, stands in Lincoln Square in Springfield. In later years it was rebuilt just as it was when Lincoln made his famous "house divided" speech there.

Probably the most visited spot at Springfield is the tomb where the 16th President and Mrs. Lincoln and three of their four sons are buried. Robert Todd Lincoln, who is buried at Arlington National Cemetery, is the only one of the Lincoln sons not buried in the tomb in Oak Ridge Cemetery at Springfield.

The citizens of Springfield organized the National Lincoln Monument Association and started a drive for funds. Construction of the tomb was started in 1869 and the memorial, costing one hundred eighty thousand dollars, was dedicated in 1874.

Abraham Lincoln is buried in Oak Ridge Cemetery in Springfield.
The tomb was designed by Larkin G. Mead and it was dedicated
in 1874. The upkeep of the tomb is handled by the state.

The cornerstone of the state capitol was laid in 1868.

Just two years later a strange event took place. A gang of counterfeiters tried to steal the body of Lincoln. They hoped to exchange the body for the freedom of one of their members who was in jail. Secret Service agents prevented them from carrying out the plot.

The main gate at the restored Fort de Chartres.

ENCHANTMENT OF CHICAGO

In the twenty-three years between its incorporation as a city and the nomination of Abraham Lincoln in the Wigwam in Chicago, that city grew from a population of 4,000 to a population of 109,260. This remarkable growth made it the "wonder city" of the country, and there are a good many citizens of Chicago today who claim it has never given up that title.

Today there is something in Chicago to attract people of almost every interest. Probably the best place to start to know Chicago is in its museums. Taken together, Chicago's museums and zoos form the finest collection in the world. Many cities have one or more great museums, but no other city has a leading museum of every one of the major types of museums, plus a multitude of similar smaller museums.

The beautiful building of the Field Museum of Natural History, overlooking the city from the edge of Grant Park, is one of the largest and finest structures in the city.

This was one of the first museums to show animals and plants as they appear in their natural settings outdoors. The museum now has one of the finest collections of these natural settings, or dioramas.

Across Lake Shore Drive from the Field Museum is the Shedd Aquarium, with one of the largest exhibits of fish. The ocean fish in the aquarium swim in natural salt water which must be brought from the ocean in tank cars.

Just to the east of the Aquarium is the Adler Planetarium, one of the most complete in the world.

The building that houses the Chicago Museum of Science and Industry was once the Fine Arts Building for the old World's Columbian Exposition. Many years after the fair, the building was rebuilt of permanent stone.

Many exhibits for this museum came from the Century of Progress Fair. They have been added to over the years. Visitors can go deep down into a "coal mine," clamber through a real German U-boat, and marvel at all the wonders of the Space Age.

The Art Institute and the Chicago Historical Society's museums are two of the finest examples of their types. The Chicago area offers not one but two of the world's leading zoos, the one in Lincoln Park, and the enormous one at Brookfield. The Brookfield Zoo is proud of its "oceanarium" away from the seacoast. Here the visitor can watch trained porpoises and other marine creatures.

Chicago is the only great city on a major body of water to have kept most of its waterfront for public use. Except for a small area near the Loop and a few private areas on the north and south sides, Chicago's entire lakefront is one long row of public parks and

*Left: Chicago has
built a world
reputation for
its outdoor civic
art by renowned
artists. Picasso's
statue in the
Daley Center has
become the city's
symbol. Below: The
Shedd Aquarium.*

Lincoln Park gardens and conservatory.

beaches. Nowhere else can so many city people find waterside recreation so close to every home.

Chicago was the birthplace of the skyscraper. Later on, the city originated two new styles of skyscrapers which are being imitated all over the country.

The first skyscraper of the type that is almost all steel and glass was built in Chicago. Most of the new buildings that have recently been put up around the world have been of the same type.

To keep its skyscraper reputation, Chicago now has the world's tallest, fourth-tallest, and fifth-tallest buildings. The 110-story Sears Tower is the tallest occupied structure in the world. The Standard Oil Building and the John Hancock Building, only a few feet below the Standard, rank fourth and fifth. The Hancock Building is the world's tallest residence. Other Chicago skyscrapers are also taller than any west of New York. Among the city's landmarks, the unusual "corn-cob" twin towers of Marina City stand out.

Perhaps the greatest single attraction of Chicago now is the North Michigan Avenue shopping center, with its 100-story Hancock and 73-story Water Tower Place buildings. Water Tower Place includes two major department stores, more than 150 other shops, three theaters, numerous restaurants, over 30 floors of apartments, the Ritz Carlton Hotel, and multi-story lobbies that constantly attract gaping crowds.

Nearby is the original Water Tower, survivor of the great Chicago Fire. The quaint structure provides welcome contrast to the glitter of the modern metropolis and serves as an information center for visitors.

Many authorities rank Chicago among the world's most dynamic, interesting, and progressive cities.

PRESERVED FOR FUN AND REMEMBRANCE

The state of Illinois now has nearly one hundred state parks and state memorials. The largest of these is Pere Marquette State Park, named in honor of Father Marquette, who camped there with his companion Louis Jolliet. Not far from Marquette Park is one of the outstanding relics of the United States. This has been preserved as Cahokia Mounds Park. The mounds are generally considered to be the most important work left by a prehistoric race in North America.

To the south is Kaskaskia Memorial. Kaskaskia, the first capital of Illinois, had the strangest fate of all. The Mississippi River cut through the narrow neck of land occupied by the town and washed

Blackhawk statue in Lowden State Park.

83

away its historic buildings. Today the Mississippi River covers most of the place where the capital of Illinois once stood.

On the island left by the river when it cut its new channel is a fine memorial building built to remember the stirring times of those early years in Illinois. The building houses the "Liberty Bell of the West." This was the bell that rang out proudly when George Rogers Clark captured the town of Kaskaskia for America. The bell is older than the famous Liberty Bell in Philadelphia.

Strangely enough, Kaskaskia Island is now the only part of Illinois west of the Mississippi River. This is true because the boundary was fixed before the river changed its course and the old boundary was kept even though the river moved.

Other well-known state parks are Starved Rock, Giant City, and Kickapoo. At Kickapoo, Indians discovered and used the salt wells. Black Hawk State Park stands where once there was the largest Indian village in North America. Now each Labor Day weekend the Indians hold a famous powwow there. Fort de Chartres State Park has partly restored this old fort, at one time the largest on the continent.

HIGH ROADS AND LOW ROADS

Springfield, of course, has many points of interest not connected with Abraham Lincoln. The first capitol building was a rented one at Kaskaskia. The present statehouse in Springfield was finished at a cost of four and a half million dollars. The capitol grounds cover 9 acres (3.6 hectares) and the building is in the form of a Latin cross. The foundation for the great dome is 92.5 feet (28.2 meters) across and is set 25.5 feet (7.7 meters) below the ground level on a bed of solid rock. Walls supporting the dome are 17 feet (5.2 meters) thick to the first story. The walls are of various kinds of limestone, from several parts of the state.

Other important state buildings at Springfield are the Centennial Building, Archives Building, Armory Building, Supreme Court Building, and Illinois State Office Building.

*The "Piasa Palisades" and other Mississippi cliffs
are among the noteworthy features of Illinois' geography.*

An Illinois building of an entirely different kind attracts a great number of visitors. This is the Baha'i Temple just north of Chicago in Wilmette. The temple takes the form of a tall dome. Its nine sides represent the nine different religions recognized by the Baha'i faith. The dome of the temple is decorated with a novel kind of concrete "lace," which was invented especially for it. The building is placed in one of the most beautiful garden settings in the entire Chicago area, with trees, flowers, and fountains. It is the United States headquarters for the Baha'i faith.

Galena is another "must" on anyone's list of places to see in Illinois. President Grant's home has been kept as a memorial in

Sunset over Mississippi Palisades State Park.

Illinois' second oldest city, and the building is open to the public. Galena's old buildings, the very hilly streets, and remembrances of the past are all tourist attractions. Galena is especially attractive in the autumn when the whole region is a riot of colorful fall foliage.

On both sides of Galena, Highway 20 becomes one of the most scenic roads in Illinois. For much of the way the road follows Terrapin Ridge, a crest of land almost level along the top. It extends for miles, sometimes through oak forests, then through clearings with deep and beautiful valleys dropping off on either side as far as the eye can see.

Another of Illinois' scenic roads is the Great River Road, following the Mississippi as closely as possible for its whole length along the Illinois border.

On this road, one of the greatest attractions is the village of Nauvoo, with its memories of the Mormons and the harsh treatment they received. After the Mormons had left, a group called the Icarians took over the town. These were similar to several other groups that started throughout the country at about this time. They believed that all property should be owned and operated by the community for the good of the members.

The Icarians started to grow grapes around Nauvoo in order to establish the wine industry that continues there. The annual grape festival draws thousands of people to Nauvoo. The Mormon organization now has restored much of old Nauvoo as a Mormon shrine.

It is claimed that the annual Easter-time Passion Play held at Bloomington was the first Passion Play in the United States. In contrast to the Passion Play, Bloomington is also the center for the training of trapeze performers. More than two hundred leading trapeze artists have trained at Bloomington since the Green brothers first practiced in a haymow and later became a featured act in Barnum's circus.

In southern Illinois are found the state's only "mountains." These hills are called the Southern Ozarks, and they attract many hunters, fishermen, and sightseers, especially in the autumn, when all the Land of Lincoln turns to Indian Summer beauty.

Handy Reference Section

Instant Facts

Became the 21st State, December 3. 1818
Capital—Springfield, founded 1821
Nickname—The Prairie State
Motto—State Sovereignty, National Union
Slogan—Land of Lincoln
State bird—Cardinal
State tree—White oak
State flower—Native violet
State song—"Illinois"
Area—56,400 square miles (146,075 square kilometers)
Rank in area—24th
Shorelines—Lake Michigan, about 61 miles (101 kilometers); Mississippi River,
            518 miles (834 kilometers); Ohio River, 113 miles (182 kilometers)
Greatest length (north to south)—381 miles (613 kilometers)
Greatest width (east to west)—211 miles (340 kilometers)
Highest point—1,235 feet (376 meters), Charles Mound
Lowest point—279 feet (85 meters), Mississpppi River
Mean elevation—600 feet (183 meters)
Number of counties—102
Population—11,418,461 (1980 census)
Rank in population—5th
Population density—202 persons per square mile (78 persons per square
            kilometer) 1980 census
Rank in density—10th
Population center—In Grundy County, 9.8 miles (15.7 kilometers) southwest of
            Morris
Birthrate—15.1 per 1,000
Infant mortality rate—20 per 1,000 births
Physicians per 100,000—151

Principal cities—		
Chicago	3,005,072	(1980 census)
Rockford	139,712	
Peoria	124,160	
Springfield	99,637	
Decatur	94,081	
Aurora	81,293	
Evanston	73,706	
East St. Louis	55,200	

You Have a Date with History

1673—Marquette and Jolliet, first Europeans in Illinois
1699—Cahokia founded, oldest town in Illinois
1703—Kaskaskia founded
1720—Fort de Chartres finished
1763—British take control of Illinois from French
1778—George Rogers Clark captures Kaskaskia
1784—Illinois becomes part of the United States
1809—Illinois made into a separate terrirory
1812—Second war with the British
1812—Fort Dearborn massacre
1814—First Illinois newspaper
1818—Illinois becomes a state
1820—Capital moved from Kaskaskia to Vandalia
1829—First college in Illinois: Illinois College, Jacksonville
1830—Lincoln family moves to Illinois
1832—Black Hawk War
1837—First iron plow invented by John Deere at Grand Detour
1839—Capital moved to Springfield
1848—First successful railroad in Illinois
1858—Lincoln-Douglas debates
1860—Lincoln elected president
1861—Civil War begins
1865—Lincoln assassinated
1869—Grant becomes president
1871—Chicago fire
1874—Lincoln Tomb dedicated at Springfield
1888—Present capitol building completed
1893—World's Columbian Exposition, Chicago
1900—Chicago River reversed
1933—Century of Progress, Chicago
1942—First controlled atomic chain reaction, Chicago
1960—Dresden nuclear power reactor completed
1966—Picasso sculpture, a gift to Chicago
1968—150th anniversary of statehood celebrated
1970—New State Constitution adopted
1971—U.S. Atomic Energy Commission National Accelerator Laboratory opens
       near Batavia
1973—World's tallest building, the Sears Tower, completed in Chicago
1976—Chicago mourns the death of long-time Mayor Richard J. Daley

Thinkers, Doers, Fighters

Men and Women Who Helped Make Illinois Great

Jane Addams
Shadrach Bond
Gwendolyn Brooks
George Rogers Clark
Richard J. Daley
John Deere
Everett M. Dirksen
Stephen A. Douglas
Ninian Edwards
Marshall Field
Enrico Fermi
Ulysses S. Grant
Black Hawk
Ernest Hemingway
Louis Jolliet
Robert Cavelier, Sieur de La Salle
Abraham Lincoln
Vachel Lindsey
Jacques Marquette

Cyrus H. McCormick
Potter Palmer
Nathaniel Pope
George Pullman
George F. Root
Carl Sandburg
Joseph Smith
Amos Alonzo Stagg
Adlai E. Stevenson
Frederick Stock
Louis Sullivan
William Ashley (Billy) Sunday
Theodore Thomas
Henri de Tonti
Montgomery Ward
Frances Willard
Henry Clay Work
Frank Lloyd Wright
Brigham Young

Governors of Illinois

Shadrach Bond 1818-1822
Edward Coles 1822-1826
Ninian Edwards 1826-1830
John Reynolds 1830-1834
William L.D. Ewing 1834
Joseph Duncan 1834-1838
Thomas Carlin 1838-1842
Thomas Ford 1842-1846
Augustus C. French 1846-1849,
  1849-1853
Joel A. Matteson 1853-1857
William H. Bissell 1857-1860
John Wood 1860-1861
Richard Yates 1861-1865
Richard J. Oglesby 1865-1869;
  Jan. 13-23, 1873; 1885-1889
John M. Palmer 1869-1873
John L. Beveridge 1873-1877
Shelby M. Cullom 1877-1881,
  1881-1883
John M. Hamilton 1883-1885

Joseph W. Fifer 1889-1893
John P. Altgeld 1893-1897
John R. Tanner 1897-1901
Richard Yates 1901-1905
Charles S. Deneen 1905-1909,
  1909-1913
Edward F. Dunne 1913-1917
Frank O. Lowden 1917-1921
Len Small 1921-1925, 1925-1929
Louis L. Emmerson 1929-1933
Henry Horner 1933-1940
John Stelle 1940-1941
Dwight H. Green 1941-1945, 1945-1949
Adlai E. Stevenson 1949-1953
William G. Stratton 1953-1957,
  1957-1961
Otto Kerner 1961-1968
Samuel H. Shapiro 1968-1969
Richard Ogilvie 1969-1973
Daniel Walker 1973-1977
James R. Thompson 1977-

90

The Chicago skyline from Lake Michigan, with Soldier Field at left, and Sears Tower, the world's tallest building.

Index

92

94

PICTURE CREDITS

Color photographs courtesy of the following: Chicago Historical Society, pages 8, 12, 16, 18, 20, 21, 23, 24, 25, 26, 29, 30, 32, 38, 40, 41, 52, 54, 58, and 66; Chicago Convention and Tourism Bureau, 81 (top) and 91; Illinois Department of Business and Economic Development, 10, 13, 62, 78, 83, 85, and 86; Illinois State Department of Conservation, 74, 77, and 79; Chicago Academy of Science, 14; Allan Carpenter, 33; Architect of the United States Capitol, 36; American Airlines, 46; Morton Arboretum, 48; Inland Steel, 56; *Peoria Journal Star* and First Federal Savings and Loan Association of Peoria, 67; University of Illinois at Urbana-Champaign, Office of Public Instruction, 70; University of Chicago, 72.

Illustrations on back cover by Len W. Meents.

ABOUT THE AUTHOR

With the publication of his first book for school use when he was twenty, **Allan Carpenter** began a career as an author that has spanned more than 135 books. After teaching in the public schools of Des Moines, Mr. Carpenter began his career as an educational publisher at the age of twenty-one when he founded the magazine *Teachers Digest*. In the field of educational periodicals, he was responsible for many innovations. During his many years in publishing, he has perfected a highly organized approach to handling large volumes of factual material: after extensive traveling and having collected all possible materials, he systematically reviews and organizes everything. From his apartment high in Chicago's John Hancock Building, Allan recalls, "My collection and assimilation of materials on the states and countries began before the publication of my first book." Allan is the founder of Carpenter Publishing House and of Infordata International, Inc., publishers of *Issues in Education* and *Index to U. S. Government Periodicals*. When he is not writing or traveling, his principal avocation is music. He has been the principal bassist of many symphonies, and he managed the country's leading non-professional symphony for twenty-five years.